I Know Someone with
Cancer

Sue Barraclough

www.raintreepublishers.co.uk
Visit our website to find out
more information about
Raintree books.

To order:

☎ Phone 0845 6044371

🖨 Fax +44 (0) 1865 312263

💻 Email myorders@raintreepublishers.co.uk

Customers from outside the UK please telephone +44 1865 312262

Raintree is an imprint of Capstone Global Library Limited,
a company incorporated in England and Wales having
its registered office at 7 Pilgrim Street, London, EC4V 6LB –
Registered company number: 6695582

Edited by Rebecca Rissman, Daniel Nunn
    and Siân Smith
Designed by Joanna Hinton Malivoire
Picture research by Mica Brancic
Originated by Capstone Global Library
Printed and bound in China by Leo Paper Products Ltd

ISBN 978 1 406 22075 9 (hardback)
15 14 13 12 11
10 9 8 7 6 5 4 3 2 1

ISBN 978 1 406 22348 4 (paperback)
16 15 14 13 12 11
10 9 8 7 6 5 4 3 2 1

British Library Cataloguing in Publication Data
Barraclough, Sue.
  I know someone with cancer. – (Understanding health
issues)
  1. Cancer–Juvenile literature.
  I. Title II. Series
  616.9'94-dc22

Acknowledgements
We would like to thank the following for permission to
reproduce photographs: Alamy p. 25 (© Stephen Lloyd
UK); Corbis pp. 14 (© Fabio Cardoso), 17 (Sygma/
Micheline Pelletier), 19 (© Kevin Dodge), 25 (© Stephen
Lloyd UK), 26 (epa/© Gero Breloer); Getty Images pp.
15 (Photographer's Choice/Mark Harmel), 16 (Stone/
David Joel); Photolibrary pp. 6 (cell division in 3d), 7 (BSIP
Medical/Raguet H), 12 (age fotostock/Frank Siteman), 13
(Jacky Chapman), 18 (BSIP Medical/Godong/Deloche),
20 (Kablonk! Kablonk!), 23 (Stockbroker), 24 (Cultura/
Christine Schneider), 27 (Tim Rooke); Science Photo Library
pp. 8 (Moredun Animal Health Ltd), 9 (Power and Syred);
Shutterstock pp. 4 (© Yuri Arcurs), 5 (Margot Petrowski), 10
(Gertjan Hooijer), 21 (© Sean Prior), 22 (Monkey Business
Images).

Cover photograph of a cancer patient reproduced with
permission of Getty Images (Taxi Japan/ULTRA.F).

We would like to thank Matthew Siegel and Ashley Wolinski
for their invaluable help in the preparation of this book.

Contents

Do you know someone with cancer? 4

What is cancer? 6

What causes cancer? 10

Understanding cancer 12

Treating cancer 14

How does it feel? 20

Being a good friend 22

What can I do? 24

Famous people with cancer 26

Cancer – true or false? 28

Glossary 30

Find out more 31

Index 32

Some words are printed in bold, **like this**. You can find out what they mean in the glossary.

Do you know someone with cancer?

You might know someone who has been ill with cancer. Someone with cancer might have treatment for a long time to make them fit and healthy again.

Someone who has cancer may have to spend a lot of time in hospital.

Cells are too small to see, but they make up every part of your body.

Cancer is a type of illness that affects the **cells** in the body. Cells are tiny living parts that fit together to make your body.

What is cancer?

Most **cells** in the body grow and divide all the time. This growth and change is controlled. This means it starts and stops to do a particular job, such as making new cells or healing cells that have been damaged.

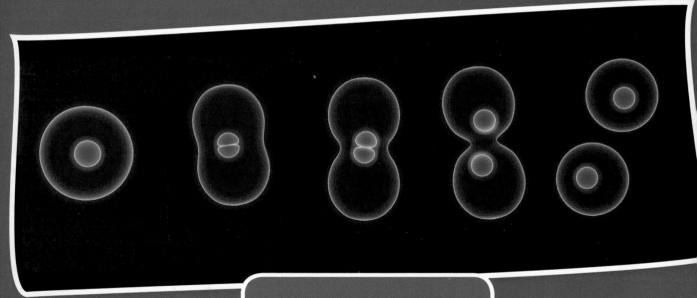

This shows how normal cells divide and grow.

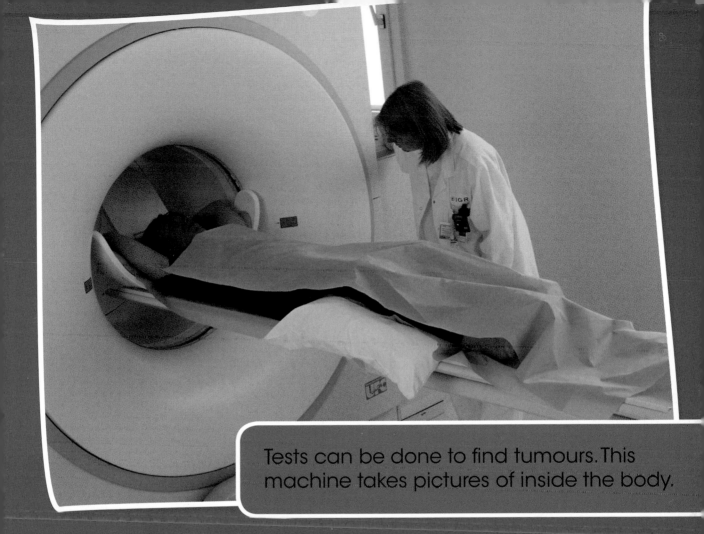

Tests can be done to find tumours. This machine takes pictures of inside the body.

Cancer is when cells start to grow out of control and divide too fast. Groups of cancer cells can cause growths called **tumours**. A tumour is a swelling or a lump caused by cells growing out of control.

Tumours happen inside the body and cannot always be seen from outside the skin.

tumour

If a **tumour** is not treated it can grow so big that it stops body parts working. Cancer **cells** can break away from some types of tumour, and spread to other parts of the body. Other types of tumour do not spread.

There are many different types of cancer. Some cancers affect a particular part of the body, such as the brain or the skin. **Leukaemia** is a type of cancer that affects white blood cells in blood. The white blood cells of people with leukaemia can't fight off illness.

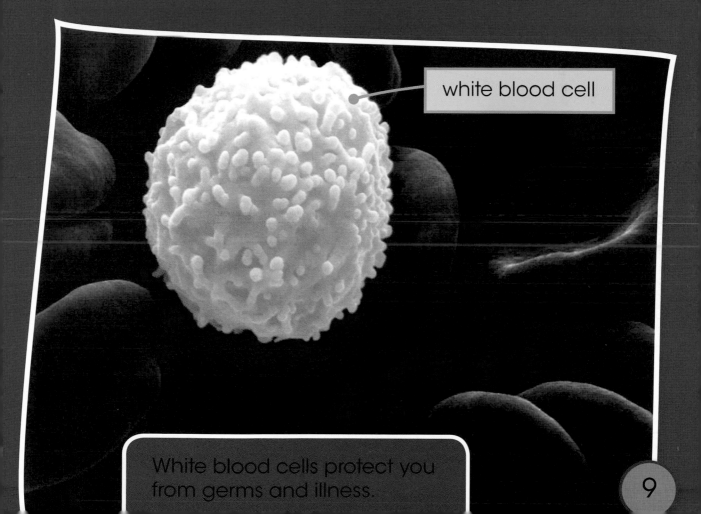

white blood cell

White blood cells protect you from germs and illness.

What causes cancer?

Smoking can cause some cancers.

Some cancers can be caused by smoking. Some may be caused by eating unhealthy food. However, the cause of many cancers is not known.

There are many ways to keep your body heathy and cut down the risk of getting cancer.

Stay healthy by:

- eating fewer fatty foods and more fruit and vegetables
- exercising every day to keep fit and healthy
- covering your skin and using sun cream when you are out in the sun
- trying not to stay in the sun for too long. Twenty minutes of sunshine is enough to keep your body healthy.

Understanding cancer

If someone in your family has cancer, it is very worrying for everyone. Some people die because their cancer is found too late and cannot be treated. But many people have treatment and survive.

There may be a lot to understand about possible treatments for cancer.

Scientists are working hard to find new and better ways to treat cancer.

When people talk about cancer, one word you might hear is '**remission**'. This means that treatment has been successful and all signs of cancer are gone from the body.

Treating cancer

Cancer can be treated by **surgery**, **chemotherapy**, or **radiation**. Sometimes one or all of the treatments are used. Surgery is when cancer **cells** are taken out of the body during an operation.

People are put into a very deep sleep before an operation so that they do not feel anything.

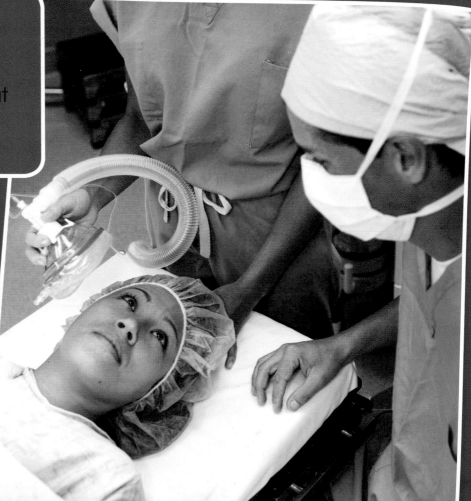

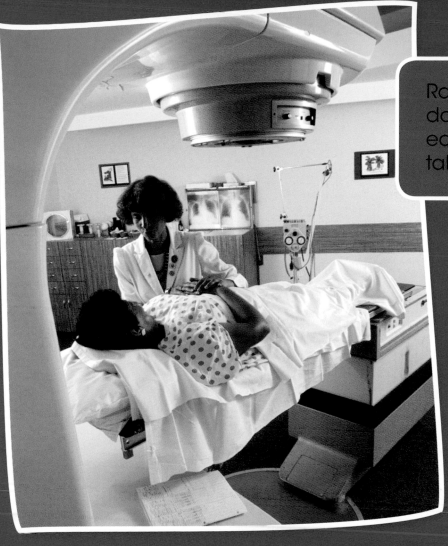

Radiation treatment
does not hurt and
each treatment only
takes a few minutes.

Radiation treatment uses special
energy to kill cancer cells and stop
tumours growing. A radiation machine
beams energy on to a part of the body
to kill cancer cells.

Chemotherapy is a treatment where medicine is put into the body to kill cancer **cells**. It is also used to try to stop cancer cells from growing or from coming back.

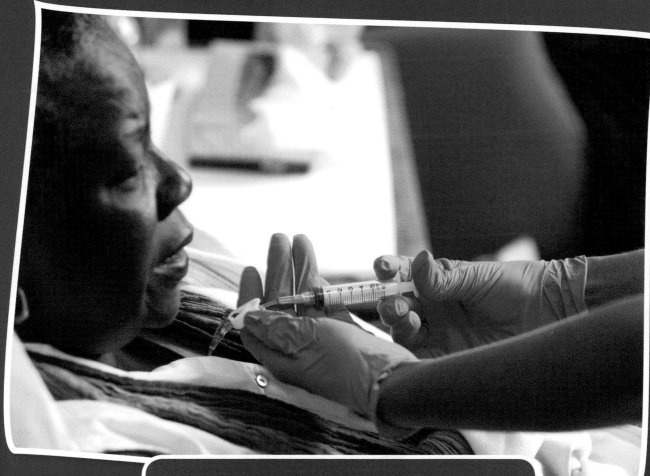

Chemotherapy and radiation are used with **surgery** to make sure all the cancer cells are destroyed.

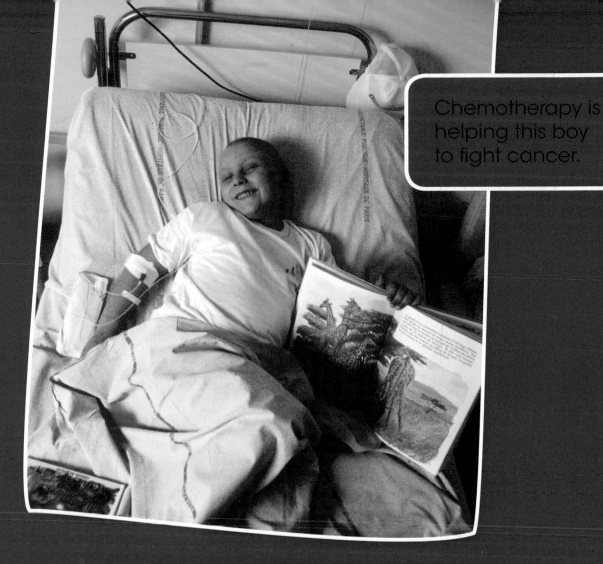

Chemotherapy is helping this boy to fight cancer.

People who have chemotherapy or **radiation** treatment may lose their hair and sometimes feel sick for a while. Their hair will grow back after the treatment has finished.

Someone who has had treatment may have to stay away from school or work for some time. This is because they are more likely to catch colds or other illnesses.

There are lots of ways of learning new things outside school.

Many people make a strong recovery from cancer.

It can take a long time for life to get back to normal after treatment has finished. But most people who have had successful treatment are able to do all the things they did before.

How does it feel?

Talking about feelings and finding out that other people feel the same way can help.

Some people with cancer feel angry that they are ill. Sometimes people feel scared. It is important to understand that all these feelings are normal.

If you know someone close to you who has cancer you may feel angry because they are ill and have to spend time in hospital. You will probably be scared or worried, too.

You do not need to hide your feelings. It is okay to feel scared.

Being a good friend

If you know someone with cancer, try to be a good friend by treating them the same. Do not worry that you will not know what to do or say, just take time to be with them.

Find things that you enjoy doing together.

A person with cancer may not want to talk about their illness. Everyone copes with illness in different ways.

Making plans will help you both look forward to the future.

Tips for helping a friend with cancer:

- Help your friend to stay cheerful. Make plans for things you can do together.

- Be there to listen if they want to talk.

What can I do?

There are many different ways you can help someone with cancer. For example, find out if there is anything you can do to help a family member who is having treatment. You may be able to help with jobs or look after younger relatives.

Having help with everyday jobs can sometimes help people to feel less anxious or scared.

Going on a sponsored walk can be a good way to raise money for charity.

Many **charities** work hard to raise money for cancer research. They use the money to try to find better treatment and **cures** for cancer. There are lots of different things you can do to help cancer charities.

Famous people with cancer

Lance Armstrong is a famous cyclist. He found out he had cancer when he was 25. He had two **surgeries** and three rounds of **chemotherapy**. Lance started the Lance Armstrong Foundation to raise money for cancer research.

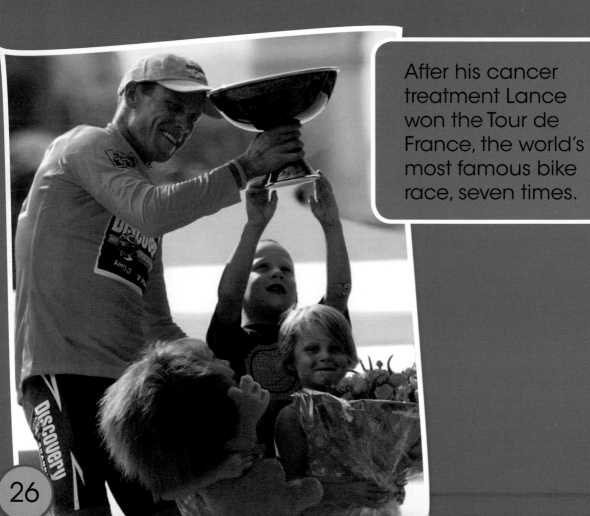

After his cancer treatment Lance won the Tour de France, the world's most famous bike race, seven times.

Kylie Minogue is a supporter of the Pink Ribbon Foundation that raises money for cancer research.

Kylie Minogue is a famous singer and actress. She found out that she had breast cancer in 2005. After surgery and a course of chemotherapy, she was in **remission**. This meant that all signs of cancer had been removed.

Cancer – true or false?

Sunscreen protects you from skin cancer.

TRUE! Sunscreen is helpful as it gives some protection against the harmful effects of the sun. It is also important not to stay in the sun for too long, and to keep skin covered up.

You can catch cancer from someone who has cancer.

FALSE! Cancer is not like a cold or flu. It cannot be passed from one person to another.

Everyone who gets cancer dies.

FALSE! Treatments for cancer are improving all the time. Many people make a very good recovery.

If your parents have cancer, then you will get cancer too.

FALSE! Some cancers do run in families, but many do not. And even with cancers that do run in families, a person can do a lot to reduce the risk of getting cancer.

Glossary

cell tiny living parts that fit together to make a body

charity organization that gives money or help to people who need it

chemotherapy using strong medicine to kill cancer cells

cure medical treatment that makes someone better

energy power that makes things move, change, or grow

leukaemia type of cancer that stops white blood cells doing their job of fighting illness

radiation treatment that uses special energy to kill cancer cells

remission time when a serious illness is better

surgery treatment involving opening up part of a person's body in order to repair something that is wrong

tumour swelling or lump caused by cells that grow in a way that is out of control

Find out more

Books to read

My Brother has Cancer, Katherine Ballard (CCLG, 2008)

What's it like? Cancer, Angela Royston, (Heinemann Library, 2005)

Websites

kidshealth.org/kid/health_problems/ cancer/cancer.html
Visit Kids Health to learn more about cancer.

www.cclg.org.uk
Find out more about cancer on this website. Follow the link to 'Information for families' then click on 'Kids, teens and young adults' to find out about support groups and more.

Index

Armstrong, Lance 26

cancer cells 7, 8, 14, 15, 16
causes of cancer 10
cells 5, 6, 7, 8, 9, 14, 15, 16
charities 25, 26, 27
chemotherapy 14, 16, 17, 26, 27
colds, catching 18
cutting the risk of cancer 11, 29

energy 15
exercise 11

families 29
famous people with cancer 26–27
feelings 20–21
food choices 10, 11
friends 22–23

hair loss 17
helping people with cancer 22–25
hospital 4, 21

leukaemia 9

Minogue, Kylie 27

radiation 14, 15, 16, 17
recovery 12, 13, 19, 29
remission 13, 27

scared, feeling 20, 21, 24
smoking 10
sponsored walks 25
staying away from school or work 18
sun, protection from 11, 28
surgery 14, 16, 26, 27

treating cancer 4, 12, 13, 14–19
tumours 7, 8, 15

what cancer is 6–9
white blood cells 9